by arrows and then beheaded. In retribution Edmund is supposed to have ... on whoever crosses th... wedding day.

EYE TO DEBEN...

Reaching Eye, visitors ... Trail, a way-marked wal... market town. Eye town ... of a motte and bailey ca... the splendid 14th century church and 15th century timbered Guildhall. We then follow narrow lanes across the heavy clay soil known as "High Suffolk " to the heights above Debenham where the river Deben rises. With a downhill rush we enter the town where the Kings of East Anglia held court in Saxon times. Picturesque timber framed buildings of the 14th and 17th century line its streets.

DEBENHAM TO FRAMLINGHAM.

We leave Debenham by following its infant river as it calls at Cretingham, Brandeston and Kettleburgh, where we leave the Deben to pursue the gentle climb to historic Framlingham. Only the walls of Framlingham's castle remain but they are one of the finest curtain fortifications in the land, built in the 12th century by the Bigods, Earls of Norfolk. The walk around its high battlements gives superb views of the old town, mere and surrounding woodlands. Framlingham town is perched on a low hill, with many attractive buildings in the streets and alleys leading off its triangular market place. Overlooking Market Hill is the impressive 14th century church, resting place of the Howard's, Lords of Framlingham. Their monuments are some of the finest renaissance stone carvings to be found in any English country church.

FRAMLINGHAM TO HALESWORTH.

From Framlingham we head north, skirting the mere as it reflects stunning views of the castle. Slowly we gain height to pass Shawsgate vineyard and then on to Cransford before riding the switchback to Bruisyard. Here we cross the river Alde, passing the regimented rows of vines of Bruisyard Vineyard. Following a narrow downhill run we ford the stream and pass the ancient church of St Peter's, before commencing the climb to Peasenhall. Descending into Peasenhall we first glimpse a row of pretty cottages lining the old Roman road. At the junction we face a Swiss chalet bequeathed to the village for use as a village hall. We cross the village brook and follow its course along Peasenhall's attractive main street as far as the village sign. Here we leave Peasenhall and cross the river Yox and navigate north to meet the young river Blyth and then follow its meandering into Halesworth.

HALESWORTH TO BUNGAY.

Built on the river Blyth, Halesworth is a pleasant market town surrounded by rural beauty. We pass through its ancient heart and see an architectural heritage dating back to the Middle Ages. At the centre of the town we pass close to the market square dominated by the adjacent church and almshouses. Crossing the Blyth by its pedestrian bridge we leave Halesworth and head uphill towards Holton's windmill. Beyond the mill's broad sails we pass east of the church and follow the perimeter of the old airfield. The trail crosses the railway and slowly twists and turns its way across the great greens of the Ilketshalls and then unexpectedly to pass the delightful ruins of Mettingham Castle. With Mettingham's eroded walls behind, we descend the Waveney valley into Bungay and follow its streets to the old market cross. From here we can explore the delights of this old riverside town, visit its ruined castle and follow the Town Trail.

WILDLIFE.

During late spring and early summer the wayside verges are laden with wildflowers. Shaded areas hide bluebells, snowdrops, wood anemone, foxglove, campion and ransoms detected afar by their sweet smell of garlic. In full sun primroses, poppy, cowslip, stitchwort, bugle, cow parsley, meadow sweet, mallow and willow herb cover the banks and margins. The hedgerow and trees which line the lanes include hawthorn, blackthorn, dog rose, bramble, sloe, cherry, chestnut, sycamore, oak, elder, ash, lime, crab apple, hazel, beech, elm, holly and willow.

The shy roe and muntjak deer are frequently seen, and small mammals abound, principally, rabbit, hedgehog, hare, weasel, grey squirrel and fox. Our native pheasant, partridge, kestrel, wood pigeon, magpie, rook, crow, yellowhammer, jay, pied wagtail, skylark and starling are ever present. While the warmer weather brings many migrating visitors, including cuckoo, martin, swallow and swift. Many species of butterfly are on the wing

between April and September especially the orange tip, small skipper, peacock, small tortoiseshell, hedge brown, meadow brown and ringlet. But, whatever the season there is always something to see, hear and wonder at.

MARKET DAYS, IN THE HEART OF SUFFOLK

Town	Early Closing	Market Days
Bungay	Wednesday	Thursday
Beccles	Wednesday	Friday
Campsea Ash	Monday	
Debenham	Tuesday	
Eye	Tuesday	Monday
Framlingham	Wednesday	Saturday
Halesworth	Thursday	Wednesday
Laxfield	Wednesday	
Mendham	Tuesday	
Needham Market	Tuesday	
Peasenhall	Wednesday	
Saxmundham	Thursday	Alt. Wed
Stowmarket	Tuesday	Thurs/Sat
Wickham Market	Wednesday	Monday

PLACES TO VISIT.

This cycling guide identifies and summarises information about the tourist attractions on and adjacent to the route. For further information about these attractions, their opening hours, admission prices etc. and all the other places of interest in Suffolk, refer to the Day Out in Suffolk guide. This free brochure is available from Tourist Information Centres throughout Suffolk.

WHERE TO STAY.

For those wishing to stay, there is a wide range of accommodation from farmhouses offering traditional bed and breakfast to fully serviced country hotels. For those who prefer to cater for themselves there is a wide selection of country holiday cottages to rent or if it's the outdoor life that you prefer there are attractive caravan and campsites. With plenty of restaurants, tearooms and pubs serving local ales, wines and cider you are promised an experience not to forget. For further information contact one of Suffolk Tourist Information Centres for details of approved hotels, B&B's, self catering accommodation, caravan and camping sites within the county.

REFRESHMENTS.

There are plenty of pubs along the route, and many restaurants and teashops in the larger villages. For those self-catering, expect to find shops only in the larger villages, see the route map for details.

PUBLIC TRANSPORT (TRAIN).

In support of an integrated transport strategy, The Heart of Suffolk Cycle Route is signed, to and from its 9 nearest railway stations, Diss, Stowmarket, Needham Market, Wickham Market, Saxmundham, Darsham, Halesworth, Brampton and Beccles.

Cycle carriage for the latest information and charges phone Anglia Railways on 01473 69 34 69. Anglia Railways **local services** have space for the carriage of 4 bikes, regrettably no tandems, advance booking is recommended to avoid disappointment as the unallocated space is sold on a first come first served basis. Some trains on the **mainline service** permit the carriage of tandems and as with bicycles advance reservation is essential on this service.

To obtain information about any service, whether in Suffolk or nationwide, phone the National Rail Enquiry service on 08457 48 49 50

PUBLIC TRANSPORT (BUS & COACH).

Bus and coach information call **TraveLine** 0645 583358 open Monday to Friday 0845 to 1800 and Saturday 0900 to 1230. **TraveLine** is Suffolk County Council's travel advice service

BY CAR.

See the detailed town maps for the recommended car parks. But before using your car consider travelling to your starting point by train, bus or cycle.

CYCLE HIRE.

This information is available from Tourist information Centres.

MAPS.

The format and page size has been devised to fit conventional cycle map pockets, provide tourist information at a glance and give a continuity page overlap. All route maps in this booklet have been specially drawn to a scale of 1:80 000 and additional inset maps give details of the key towns and villages.

Because the maps in this guide show only a narrow band either side of the route, you are advised to take with you the appropriate Ordnance Survey Landranger map, number 156 Saxmundham. It will provide greater area detail, enable detours and identify the various road types on and about the route.

FOLLOWING THE SIGNED ROUTE.

- The main circular route is signed in both directions.
- Look for, and follow, the signs at each junction.
- If no signs are present then follow the road you are on.
- Do not cross the white lines of adjoining roads unless indicated by route signs.

MISSING ROUTE SIGNS

The route is checked regularly, but occasionally signs are damaged or wilfully removed. If you are aware of missing signs please write to or phone:

The Heart of Suffolk Cycle Route, Suffolk County Council, Environment and Transport Dept. St Edmund House, County Hall, Ipswich IP4 1LZ. Telephone 01473 583202. e-mail cycle.info@et.suffolkcc.gov.uk

DAY RIDES. (UNSIGNED)

For the more adventurous cyclists, unsigned circular and cross-route short cuts have been mapped and included within the guide. This will to enable you to prepare your own ride itinerary and explore the secret Heart of Suffolk. These additional routes use quiet lanes and visit other villages of interest and appeal, and where many of the Heart of Suffolk walks begin.

BE SAFE.

- Make sure your bicycle is in good working order. Test brakes, wheels and tyres.
- Be seen wear bright reflective colours.
- Both adults and children are advised to wear a cycle helmet.
- Be prepared, always carry a first aid kit, small tool kit, puncture repair kit, spare inner tube and pump.
- Take special care when cycling downhill, especially on corners where vehicles could be approaching unseen
- Follow the advice given in the Highway Code and let other road users know your intentions, by giving clear arm signals.
- Ride in single file on busy roads.
- Although the Heart of Suffolk route follows mostly small lanes it crosses and joins a number of main roads. Care should be taken at all times. Preferably stop at all junctions until you are sure it's safe to proceed.
- Watch out for farm machinery on country lanes.

CONSIDERATION FOR OTHERS.

- Always give way to horse riders and walkers, and remember that some people have impaired hearing or sight.
- Warn them of your approach, whistle, call out or best of all fit a bell and use it.

SECURITY.

- To prevent theft of your bicycle, always lock it to a fixed object and remove lights, pump and valuables.
- Keep a note of your bicycle frame number, its colour, make and model.

ACCIDENTS.

In event of an accident, you should note the following.

- Name and address of others involved.
- Registration number of vehicle(s) involved.
- Time and place of accident.
- Name and address of witnesses.
- If any one is hurt, or property damaged, report the incident to the police within 24 hours, and record the time date and which Police Station.
- Take a photograph of the accident site.

To telephone the emergency services, Police, Ambulance and Fire Service in the UK dial 999 from any public, mobile or private phone.

FOLLOW THE COUNTRY CODE.

- Leave livestock, and crops and machinery alone.
- Help to keep all water clean.
- Protect wildlife, plants and trees.
- Take special care on country roads.
- Make no unnecessary noise.
- Enjoy the countryside and respect its life and work.
- Guard against all risks of fire.
- Fasten all gates.
- Take your litter home.
- Keep to public paths across farmland.
- Use gates and stiles to cross fences, hedges and walls.

OTHER CYCLE LINKS.

The Heart of Suffolk Cycle route joins the National Cycle Route 1 and The Suffolk Coastal Cycle route and accesses several other published cycle routes.

For information contact any Suffolk Tourist Information Centre.

THE NATIONAL CYCLE NETWORK.

The National Cycle Network project is being co-ordinated by the charity Sustrans and it aims to provide an 8000-mile network of cycle routes by 2005.

For further information contact Sustrans, 35 King Street, Bristol, BS1 4DZ Telephone 0179 29 08 88.

THE SUFFOLK COASTAL CYCLE ROUTE.

Is a signed cycle tour around the attractive coastal region of Suffolk and its route map is available from Tourist Information Centres or Suffolk Connections 01473 584554.

PEDESTRIAN AND EQUESTRIAN LINKS.

Bridleways and footpaths abound in the county and the Heart of Suffolk Project has published a collection of way-marked equestrian trails and walks. Both these publications are available from Tourist Information Centres in Suffolk.

FRIARS TO FLYERS.

Located within the Heart of Suffolk, this aptly named project combines three historical themes. all of which have helped shape Suffolk's landscape during the last millennium. A series of leaflets and exhibitions allows you to explore many of the archaelogical remains of suffolk's medieval Friaries and Priories, it's wealth of moated Manor Houses and world War Two airfields. For more information on this exciting project phone the Project Officer on 01473 583179.

UPPER WAVENEY VALLEY COUNTRYSIDE PROJECT.

This major project covers 43 parishes in both Norfolk and Suffolk, with a combined area of 125 miles, from the source of the river Waveney at Redgrave to Bungay. Pocket parks are being developed along the valley, together with improved wheelchair access and restoration of the river course. There are plans to construct fishing platforms and launch slipways for canoes, plus six circular way-marked walks, a 40 kilometre equestrian route and cycle hire at Bungay. For more information phone the Project Officer on 01379 788008.

TOURIST INFORMATION CENTRES

Aldeburgh* 01728 453637
Beccles* 01502 713196
Bury St Edmunds 01284 764667
Felixstowe 01394 276770
Ipswich 01473 258070
Lavenham* 01787 248207
Lowestoft 01502 523000
Newmarket 01638 667200
Sudbury* 01787 881320
Southwold* 01502 724729
Stowmarket. 01449 676800
Woodbridge 01394 382240

* Seasonal opening only

LEGAL DISCLAIMER.

The identification of a specific cycle route by the erection of way-mark signs does not necessarily signify any special protection or privilege for cyclists. There is always some risk involved in using public roads, Waveney, Suffolk Coastal and Mid Suffolk District Councils and Suffolk County Council and their contractors cannot accept liability of loss or injury caused to any person following the route.

While every effort has been made to ensure that the information in this guide is correct Waveney, Suffolk Coastal and Mid Suffolk District Councils and Suffolk County Council and their contractors cannot accept responsibility for any loss due to errors or omissions, which may have occurred.

WE NEED YOUR HELP.

Please tell us how you think this booklet can be improved. Advise us of any inaccuricies so they can be corrected in future editions. Please write to Anthony Wright, Heart of Suffolk Recreational Tourism Project.Orchard House, Hawk End Lane, Elmswell, Suffolk IP30 9ED.

Funding
Waveney District Council
Suffolk Coastal District Council
Mid Suffolk District Council
Suffolk County Council
European Regional Development Fund
Rural Development Fund

Production Credits
Stirling Surveys
Graphics Matter Ltd

Concept, Research, Original Text and Project Co-ordination Credits
Anthony Wright

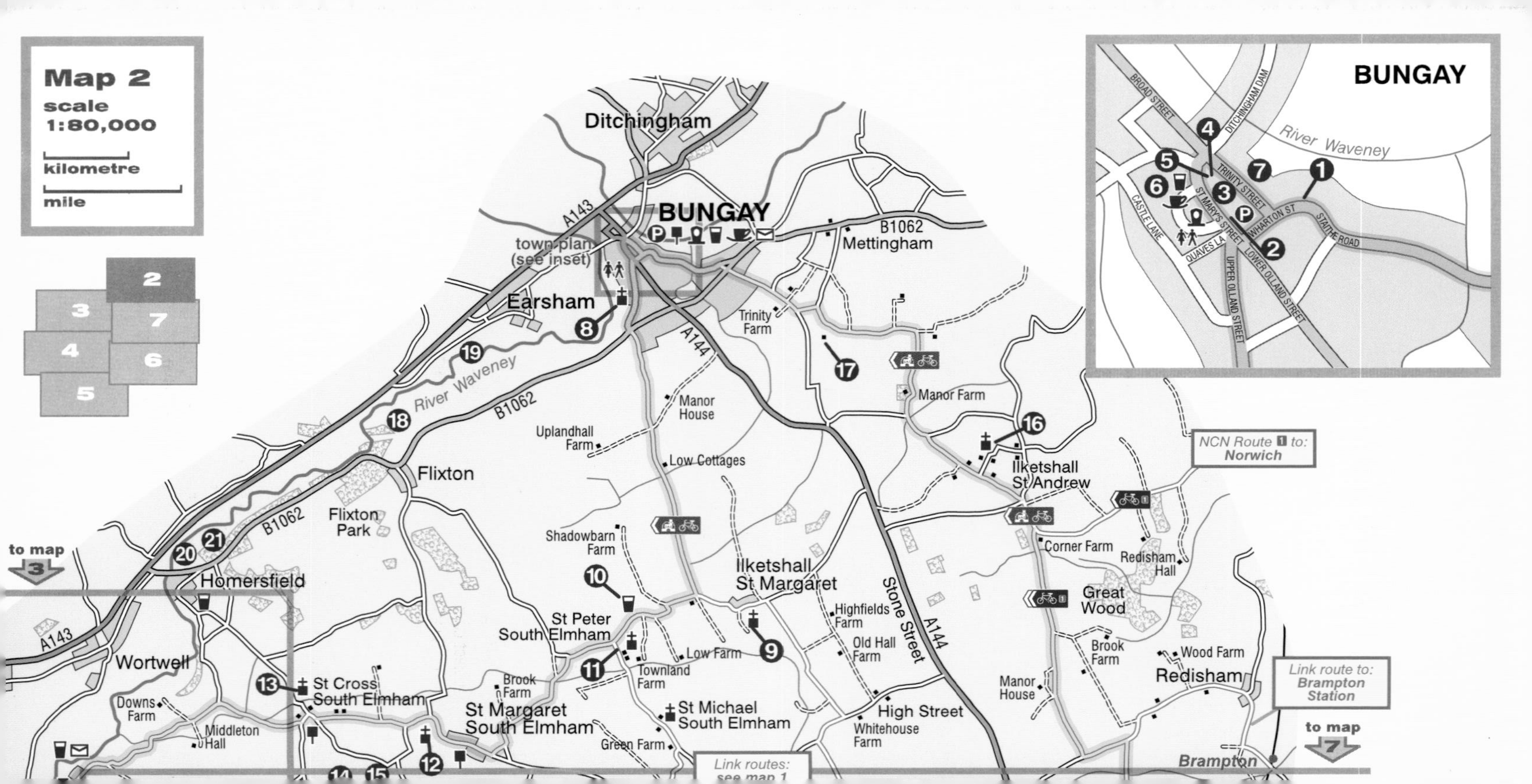
Map 2
scale
1:80,000
kilometre
mile
2
3
7
4
6
5
BUNGAY
BROAD STREET
DITCHINGHAM DAM
River Waveney
TRINITY STREET
ST MARY'S STREET
WHARTON ST
STAITHE ROAD
CASTLE LANE
QUAVES LA
UPPER OLLAND STREET
LOWER OLLAND STREET
Ditchingham
BUNGAY
A143
town plan (see inset)
Earsham
B1062
Mettingham
Trinity Farm
A144
River Waveney
B1062
Manor House
Upland hall Farm
Low Cottages
Manor Farm
Flixton
Flixton Park
NCN Route 1 to: Norwich
Ilketshall St Andrew
Corner Farm
Redisham Hall
Great Wood
Shadowbarn Farm
Ilketshall St Margaret
Stone Street
A144
Highfields Farm
Old Hall Farm
to map 3
Homersfield
A143
Wortwell
St Peter South Elmham
Low Farm
Townland Farm
St Cross South Elmham
Brook Farm
St Margaret South Elmham
St Michael South Elmham
Green Farm
High Street
Whitehouse Farm
Manor House
Brook Farm
Wood Farm
Redisham
Link route to: Brampton Station
to map 7
Brampton
Downs Farm
Middleton Hall
Link routes: see map 1

The Butter Cross, Bungay

BUNGAY

The old market town of Bungay is built around the ruins of castles built by the Norman's on a hill over looking the Waveney. Williams de Noyers raised the original castle mound in 1070. His successor Hugh Bigod built his castle in 1165, but after rebelling against Henry II in 1174 it was seized along with his castle at Framlingham. In 1294 Roger Bigod used the stone from the old castle to build his fortress with ribbon walls and the gate towers that still remain. Bungay is older than the Normans, and still today the principal town person holds the Saxon office of Reeve. In 1577 during a terrible thunderstorm, the steeple of St Mary's was hit by lightening and the Devil in the form of a black dog appeared in the church. According to legend, the devil dog swept through the church killing two and scattering all who sheltering within. The black dog known locally as 'Black Shuck' is now the emblem on the town's coat of arms and tops the weather vane in the market place. The town largely rebuilt after the great fire of 1688, contains many fine Georgian buildings including the domed octagon Butter Cross. It is from here many of the town's historic walks, and cycle routes begin. Markets are still held in the shadow of the old market cross on Thursday's.

THE SAINTS.

Collectively the six **South Elmham** parishes together with the four **Ilketshall's** are known as the "Saints". The name "Ilkeshall" is derived from the ownership of the Saxon Warlord Ulfcytel who fought the Dane Sweyn in a bloody battle near Thetford in 1004. South Elmham is steeped in history, at St.Cross, part of 13th century **Bishop's Palace** is visible in the structure of South Elmham Hall. Close by is the ruins of the 11th century **Minster,** thought to be the remains of a collegiate foundation for priests. Built at the heart of the ancient deanery of South Elmham in 675 as an extension of the Bishopric of Dunwich.

St.Cross Farm Walks offers way-marked walking routes though its mixed farm and historic countryside.

METTINGHAM CASTLE.

Sir John de Norwich was granted a licence by Edward III in 1342 to castellate his residence at Mettingham as a reward for his services in the French wars. Little now remains but for its tall Gatehouse and decaying ribbon walls.

Bungay Castle

PLACES OF INTEREST.

Bungay

01 Almshouses.
02 Angel & Dinky's Garden.
03 St.Edmunds Church.
04 St.Mary & Priory Remains.
05 Butter Cross.
06 Castle Remains.
07 Holy Trinity Church.
08 Emanuel Church.

Ilketshall St. Margaret.

09 St. Margaret's Church.

South Elmham St Peter.

10 St. Peters Hall & Brewery.
11 St.Peters Church. South Elmham

St.Margaret.

12 St.Margarets Church

South Elmham St.Cross.

13 St.George's Church.
14 The Minster, remains.
15 Bishops Palace, remains and South Elmham Hall, Farm Walks.
16 **Ilketshall,** St.Andrew's Church.
17 **Mettingham,** Castle Ruins
18 **Flixton,** Air Museum.
19 **Earsham,** Otter Trust.
20 **Homersfield,** Bridge.
21 **Homersfield,** Barnfield Cottages

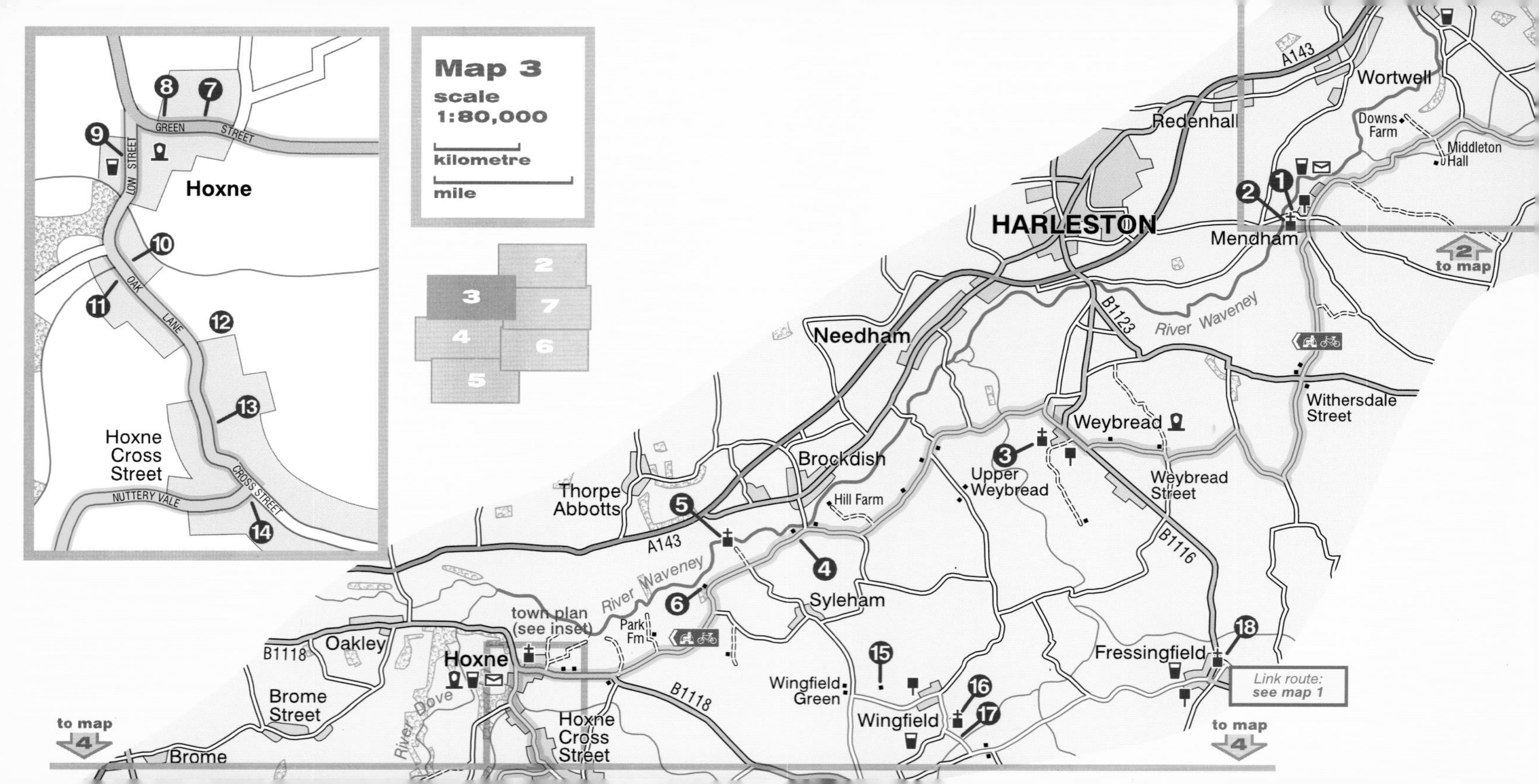

Map 3
scale
1:80,000
kilometre
mile
Hoxne
GREEN STREET
LOW STREET
OAK LANE
CROSS STREET
NUTTERY VALE
Hoxne Cross Street
HARLESTON
Redenhall
Wortwell
Downs Farm
Middleton Hall
Mendham
to map 2
A143
B1123
River Waveney
Needham
Withersdale Street
Weybread
Upper Weybread
Weybread Street
Brockdish
Hill Farm
Thorpe Abbotts
B1116
Syleham
town plan (see inset)
Park Fm
Oakley
B1118
Hoxne
River Dove
Brome Street
Brome
Hoxne Cross Street
Wingfield Green
Wingfield
Fressingfield
Link route: see map 1
to map 4
to map 4

MENDHAM.

Mendham is a pleasant village on the banks of the Waveney; it is linked to Norfolk and the outside world by its distinctive iron bridge. The bridge was built as a temporary measure by Suffolk and Norfolk County Councils, to replace the former wooden bridge lost to the floods of 1912. Not far from the bridge stands the 14th century village church of All Saints.

Sir Alfred Munnings, artist and former president of the Royal Academy, was born at Mendham Mill in 1878 the second son of the miller. He was to become the greatest English painter of horses since Stubbs. The village is dominated by his memory. The hotel bears his name and his painting called Charlotte and her pony was the inspiration for the village sign. **All Saints,** Mendham's 14th century church has in its flint tower, trefoil windows and supporting buttresses. Within the church there are three interesting portrait brasses of the 17th century Friston family, the finest is of Cecily hands clasped in prayer.

SYLEHAM.

Pronounced "sylum" the village name is derived from the Saxon word for "muddy place". In 1842 the existing water mill was converted into a cloth-mill producing linen and cotton, the manufacture of clothing continued until its closure in 1990. The mill has now been converted into dwellings with a unique river frontage.

Linked to the road by a narrow raised causeway **St.Mary's,** stands on the marshy banks of the Waveney. It was here that the rebellious Hugh Bigod surrendered his castles to Edward II in 1174. **Monks Hall** is a fine 16th century timber framed building with projecting wing ending in a brick stepped gable

HOXNE

HOXNE is not pronounced "Hoxney" but surprisingly "Hoxen", its curious name is thought to mean a hock shaped piece of land. At the top of the hill overlooking the village stands the elegant church with its embattled tower soaring almost 100 feet into the sky. A fine mixture of thatched and tiled cottages and houses are built about Hoxne's narrow sloping green. **Goldbrook Bridge** is where according to legend, King Edmund was captured by the Danes, and then tied to a nearby oak. He was told that if he renounced his Christian faith, his life would be spared. His refusal was met with a volley of Danish arrows and then the dying King was beheaded. Edmunds oak fell in 1848 and was replaced with a marble cross that bears the inscription "St.Edmund, King and Martyr, November 20th, AD 870. Oak Tree fell August 1848, by its own weight."

Edmunds body was first buried at Abbey Farm before being moved to Bury St Edmunds 33 years later.

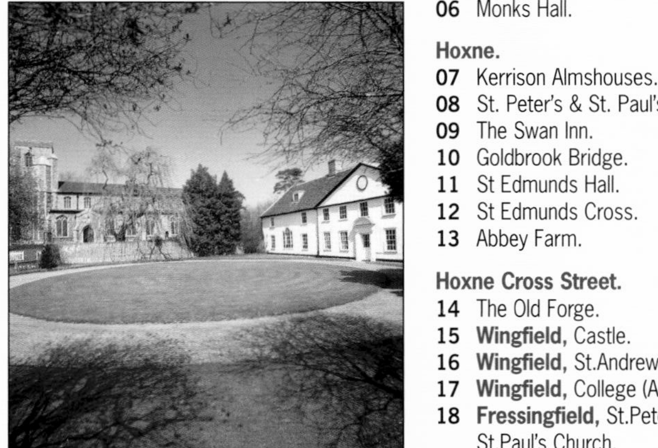

Wingfield College

PLACES OF INTEREST.

Mendham
- **01** Sir Alfred Munnings Country Hotel.
- **02** All Saints Church.

Weybread.
- **03** St Andrew's Church.

Syleham.
- **04** Old Linen Mill & Weir.
- **05** St Mary's Church.
- **06** Monks Hall.

Hoxne.
- **07** Kerrison Almshouses.
- **08** St. Peter's & St. Paul's Church.
- **09** The Swan Inn.
- **10** Goldbrook Bridge.
- **11** St Edmunds Hall.
- **12** St Edmunds Cross.
- **13** Abbey Farm.

Hoxne Cross Street.
- **14** The Old Forge.
- **15** **Wingfield,** Castle.
- **16** **Wingfield,** St.Andrew's Church.
- **17** **Wingfield,** College (Arts Centre).
- **18** **Fressingfield,** St.Peter's and St.Paul's Church.

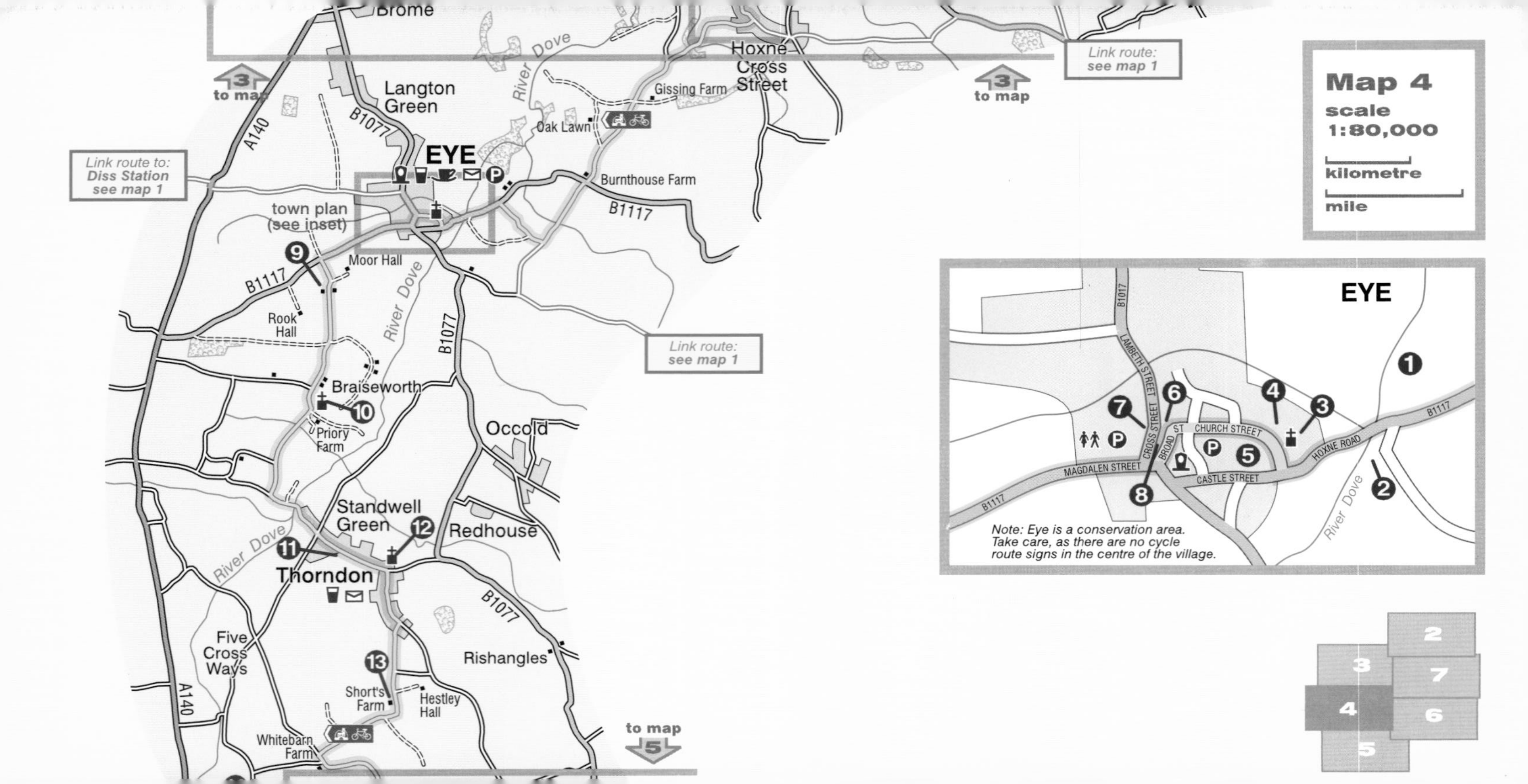

Map 4
scale
1:80,000
kilometre
mile
Brome
Langton Green
B1077
EYE
Link route to: Diss Station see map 1
town plan (see inset)
Moor Hall
B1117
Rook Hall
Braiseworth
Priory Farm
River Dove
B1077
Occold
Standwell Green
Redhouse
Thorndon
Five Cross Ways
A140
Rishangles
Short's Farm
Hestley Hall
Whitebarn Farm
to map 5
to map 3
Hoxne Cross Street
Gissing Farm
Oak Lawn
Burnthouse Farm
Link route: see map 1
EYE
B1017
LAMBETH STREET
CROSS STREET
BROAD ST
CHURCH STREET
CASTLE STREET
MAGDALEN STREET
HOXNE ROAD
Note: Eye is a conservation area. Take care, as there are no cycle route signs in the centre of the village.

Eye Guildhall and Church

EYE.

After the Norman Conquest the Honour of Eye was given to William Malet. He made Eye his power base and began building the castle, later his son Robert founded the Benedictine Priory. The castle was rebuilt and strengthened in 1182 after repelling the forces of Hugh Bigod in 1173. Attacked again in 1265, the castle was left in ruins and its remaining structure used as a prison. In 1561 a windmill was built on the castle mound and remained there until it was demolished in 1844. In its place General Sir Edward Kerrison built a cottage with the appearance of a castle. The cottage survived until it was damaged by a freak storm in 1960.

Eye's name is derived from the Saxon word for island. When the Saxons colonised the area they built a fortified encampment on the high ground surrounded by marshes and the river Dove. Eye is an attractive town with splendid houses dating from the 15th century, a magnificent church and Old Guildhall. Many changes have occurred this century but Eye still retains the air and character of a small market town. Eye has declined from its halcyon days of the 1850's. At this time there were many thriving local industries; an iron foundry, flax works, lace making a number of breweries, over twenty public houses and a host of traders supplying the family needs. But Eye's commercial importance began to decline when the railway reached Diss in 1849. Eleven years later a branch line linked Eye to Mellis but the damage to trade was irreversible. Sadly the passenger service closed in 1931 and the goods service ended in 1964. **Braisworth,** is little gem of a church has been converted into a private dwelling. Built in 1857, designed by E.B Lamb in neo-Norman style to replace the ruined church approximately half a mile to the east.

Thorndon is the site of a Bronze age settlement, many of the finds are in the British Museum. Within the parish there are many splendid old cottages and farmsteads. All Saints, the parish church is surrounded by a ring of elms. Its 14th century bell-tower is offset and stands in front of the Nave, within the tower arch a wooden staircase leads to the bell loft. Shortt's Farm south of the main settlement is a delightful half-timbered building with an elaborate stepped gable.

Eye

PLACES OF INTEREST

Eye.

01 Remains Of Priory.
02 Pennings Picnic Area.
03 St.Peter's & St.Paul's Church.
04 Old Guildhall.
05 Castle.
06 Town Hall.
07 Queens Head.
08 Kerrision Memorial.

Braisworth.

09 Rook Hall Farm.
10 Redundant Church, St.Mary's.

Thorndon.

11 The Black Horse Inn.
12 All Saints.
13 Shortt's Farm.

Brockford.

14 Mid Suffolk Light Railway Museum.

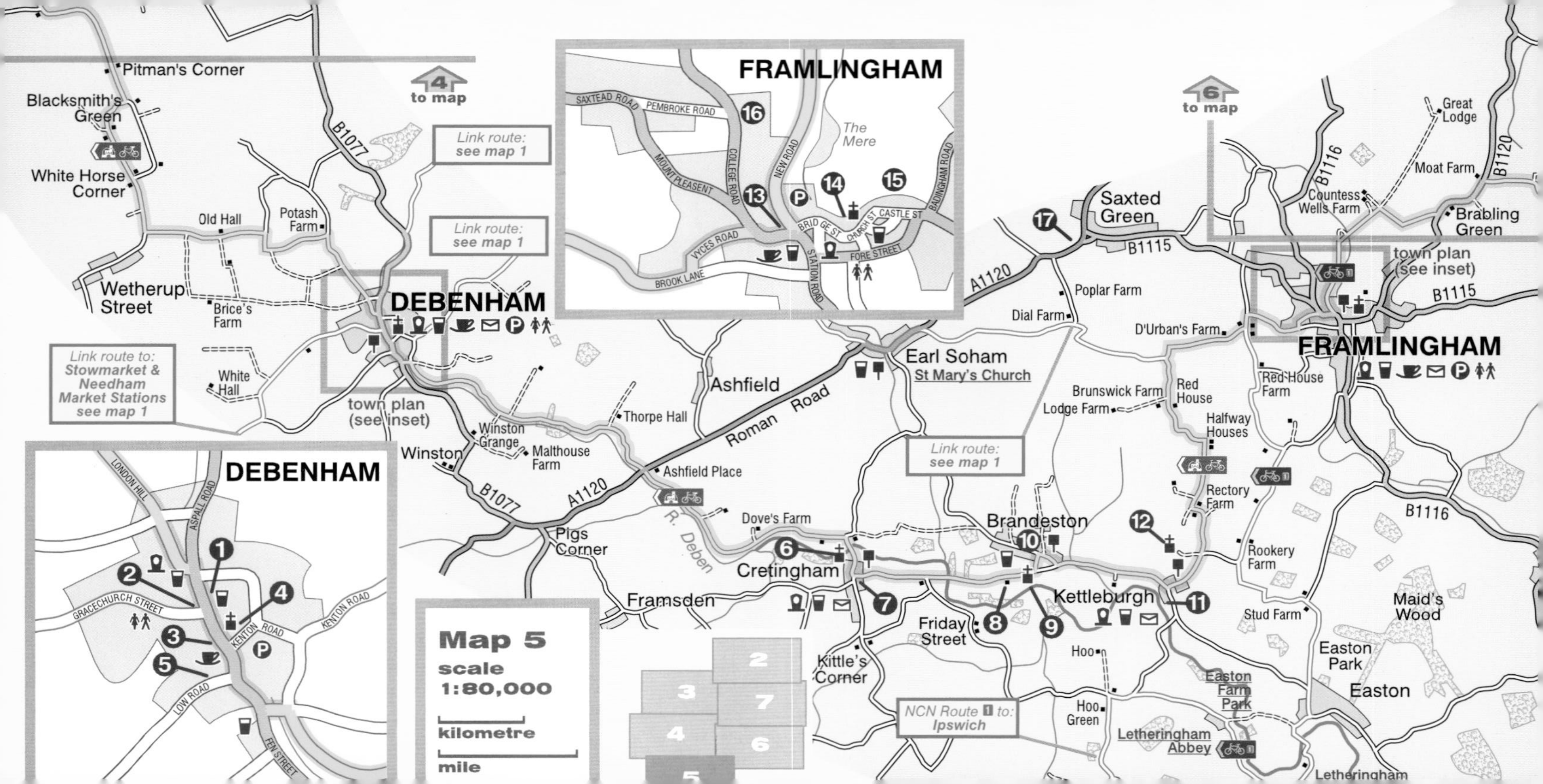
Map 5
scale
1:80,000
kilometre
mile
FRAMLINGHAM
DEBENHAM
4 to map
6 to map
Pitman's Corner
Blacksmith's Green
White Horse Corner
Old Hall
Potash Farm
Wetherup Street
Brice's Farm
White Hall
Link route: see map 1
Link route: see map 1
Link route to: Stowmarket & Needham Market Stations see map 1
town plan (see inset)
Winston
Winston Grange
Malthouse Farm
Thorpe Hall
Ashfield
Ashfield Place
Roman Road
Pigs Corner
Framsden
Dove's Farm
R. Deben
Cretingham
Kittle's Corner
Friday Street
Earl Soham
St Mary's Church
Link route: see map 1
Brandeston
Kettleburgh
Hoo
Hoo Green
NCN Route 1 to: Ipswich
Letheringham Abbey
Easton Farm Park
Easton Park
Easton
Maid's Wood
Stud Farm
Rookery Farm
Rectory Farm
Halfway Houses
Red House
Brunswick Farm
Lodge Farm
Dial Farm
Poplar Farm
D'Urban's Farm
Red House Farm
Saxted Green
Countess Wells Farm
Moat Farm
Great Lodge
Brabling Green
town plan (see inset)
Letheringham
B1077
A1120
B1115
B1116
B1120
SAXTEAD ROAD
PEMBROKE ROAD
MOUNT PLEASENT
COLLEGE ROAD
NEW ROAD
The Mere
BADINGHAM ROAD
CASTLE ST
CHURCH ST
BRIDGE ST
FORE STREET
STATION ROAD
VYCES ROAD
BROOK LANE
LONDON HILL
ASPALL ROAD
GRACECHURCH STREET
KENTON ROAD
LOW ROAD
FEN STREET
2
3
7
4
6
5

Debenham

DEBENHAM

The village gets its name from the river Deben that rises in nearby fields, after passing through the village, meanders to Woodbridge and then onto the sea. At Debenham the East Anglian Kings were reported to have held occasional court. The Domesday record of 1086 lists more people at Debenham than anywhere else in Suffolk suggesting its economic importance. Today this large village reminds us of its past prosperity through its old houses, fine buildings and church. On the brow of a hill surrounded by cottages stands the village church of St.Mary Magdalene. The base of the tower is Saxon and built more as a fortress than a place of worship, with walls four feet thick and two defensive inward splayed slit windows. The 14th century tower above houses a peal of eight bells which are thought by many to be the best in the land.

Crettingham, St.Peter is the 12th century parish church, with monuments to the Cornwallis family. The village is best remembered for the murder of its aging Vicar, the Rev. William Meymott Farley in 1887. Whose throat was cut while he slept by his demented Curate, the Rev. A.E Gilbert-Cooper.

Brandeston. Belief and fear of witchcraft was strong in Suffolk during the 17th century, Brandeston's vicar the Rev. John Lowes, was accused by the Witchfinder General, Matthew Hopkins. Lowes, was found guilty and hanged at Bury St.Edmunds, he walked to the scaffold reciting his own burial service.

Framlingham is an ancient market town perched on a low hill, with many attractive buildings in the streets and alleys leading off its triangular Market Hill. Overlooking the market place is the impressive 14th century church, dedicated to St. Michael, its resting place for the Howard's Lords of Framlingham.

The castle walls we see today are little changed from when they were built in 1199. Built to include lessons learnt in the crusades, steep defensive earthworks tall ribbon walls, protruding towers and fortified gatehouse. It was here in 1553 that Bloody Mary's supporters flocked, in only a few days, thirteen thousand men at arms encamped about the castle. Within a fortnight she began her triumphal march to London and proclaimed queen on 16th July. She was crowned amid great splendour on 1st October 1553 and reigned for 5 years and 122 days.

Framlingham Castle

PLACES OF INTEREST.

Debenham.
- **01** Former Guildhall.
- **02** Former Hitcham School.
- **03** Former Forresters Hall.
- **04** St.Mary's, Church.
- **05** Tea Pot Pottery.

Crettingham.
- **06** St.Peter's, Church.
- **07** The Bell.

Brandeston.
- **08** Brandeston Hall (School).
- **09** All Saints.
- **10** The Queens Head.

Kettleburgh.
- **11** The Chequers.
- **12** St.Andrews, Church.

Framlingham.
- **13** Hitcham Almshouses.
- **14** St.Michael's Church.
- **15** Castle.
- **16** Framlingham College.
- **17** Saxted. Post Mill.

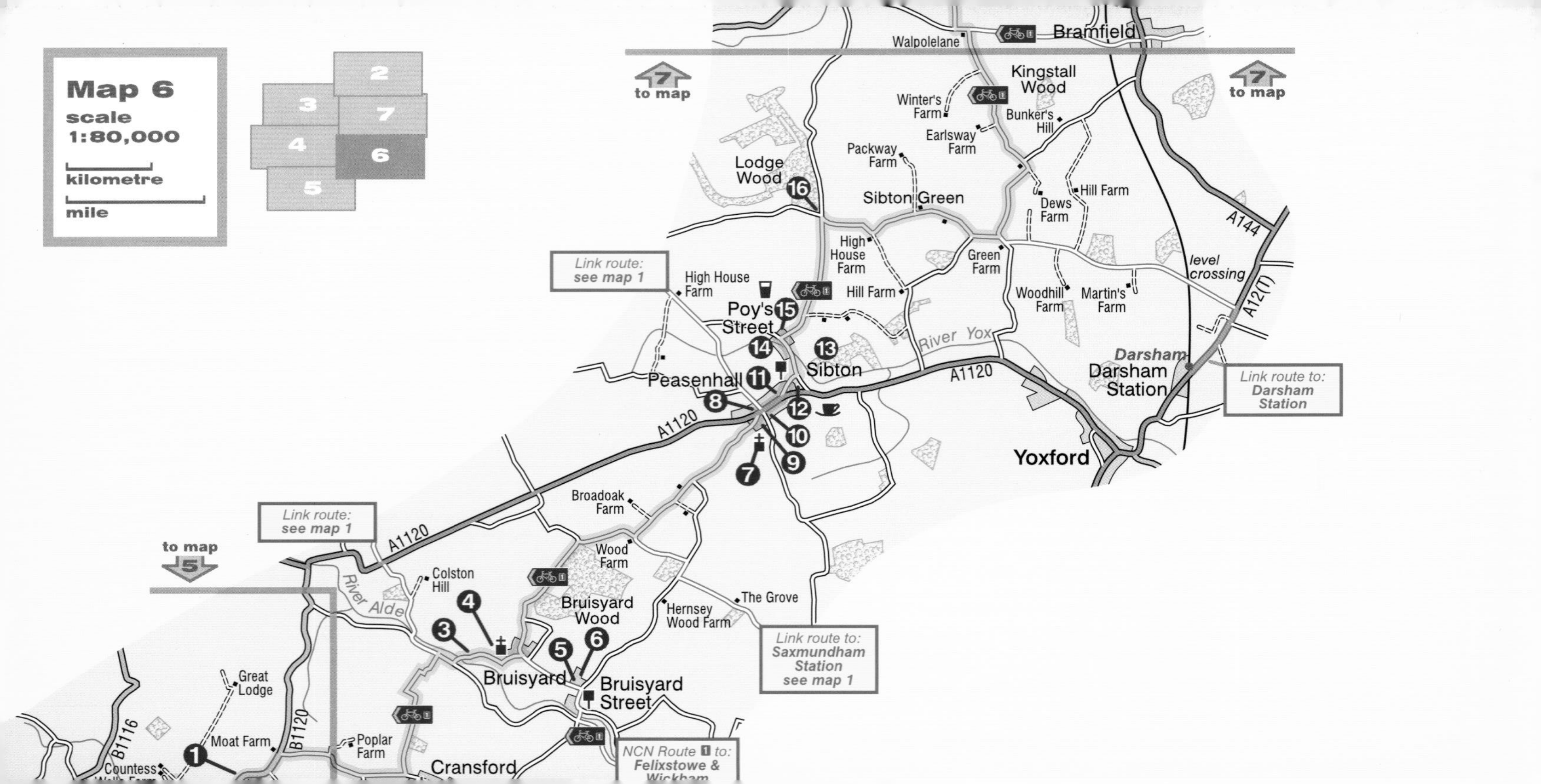

Map 6
scale
1:80,000
kilometre
mile
2
3
7
4
6
5
to map 7
to map 7
to map 5
Bramfield
Walpolelane
Kingstall Wood
Winter's Farm
Bunker's Hill
Earlsway Farm
Packway Farm
Lodge Wood
Sibton Green
Hill Farm
Dews Farm
A144
High House Farm
Green Farm
level crossing
Link route: see map 1
High House Farm
Hill Farm
Woodhill Farm
Martin's Farm
A12(T)
Poy's Street
River Yox
Sibton
Peasenhall
A1120
Darsham
Darsham Station
Link route to: Darsham Station
Yoxford
Broadoak Farm
Link route: see map 1
A1120
Wood Farm
Colston Hill
River Alde
Bruisyard Wood
Hernsey Wood Farm
The Grove
Link route to: Saxmundham Station see map 1
Great Lodge
Bruisyard
Bruisyard Street
B1116
Moat Farm
B1120
Poplar Farm
Cransford
NCN Route 1 to: Felixstowe & Wickham
Countess

CRANSFORD

Higher in elevation than its illustrious neighbour Framlingham overlooks the Alde valley. The tiny village church of St.Peter, with tower nave and chancel, was almost completely rebuilt by the Victorians in 1864. Church Farm, stands at the rear of the church and dates from 1620.

Bruisyard lies in the pleasant pastures of the Alde valley, with an old moated manor, vineyard and a little Norman church with a round tower. The flint round tower of St.Peters has older foundations and was probably first built as a defensive structure to cover the ford in the river Alde below.

Peasenhall's village street is very spacious and shaded by many mature trees. There is a watercourse, the Yoxford Brook, running down its length. South of the stream a grass bank fronts the narrow roadway "The Causeway", with its mixture of cottages and houses. The north side is lined with commercial properties and old cottages and in particular **Emmett's Stores** who produce the most succulent smoked and picked hams and hold a Royal Warrant. Further along the Street is the **Weavers Tearooms** a welcome stop to the cyclist. Peasenhall's recent past is dominated by two things, agricultural machinery and murder. The Drill Works was founded in 1800

Bruisyard Hall

and in its heyday offered employment for about four hundred men.

But the event that this sleepy Suffolk village is best remembered is the unsolved murder of Rose Harsent on 1st June 1902. Rose was in service at Providence House and it was here early on that fateful Sunday, before the house awoke, that her father discovered her body.He had entered by the kitchen door to find his daughter lying in a pool of blood with her throat cut. Rose was twenty-three years old, single and six months pregnant. Her violent death shook the close village of Peasenhall and no less shocking was the implication of William Gardiner, a married Primitive Methodist Sunday School Superintendent. During the previous year their names had been scandalously linked. Gardiner was arrested and tried twice over for the crime, in both cases the jury could not agree and he was finally released, without conviction.

Ancient House is where Julian Tennyson lived when he wrote Suffolk Scene, his descriptive pre-war narrative of Suffolk its people and places.

Sibton is an elongated parish with its village church on the extreme eastern edge, looks across the B1120 towards the Abbey remains and the river Yox. In 1150, William de Chesney founded the Cistercian Abbey of the Blessed Virgin Mary, in fulfilment of a vow to his dying brother in atonement for his sins.

PLACES OF INTEREST

01 Shawsgate Vinyard, Framlingham.

Cransford.
02 St.Peter's, Church.

Bruisyard.
03 St.Peter's Vineyard.
04 St.Peter's, Church.
05 Wayside Cross, stump off.
06 Bruisyard Hall

Peasenhall.
07 St.Peter's Church.
08 Reading Room's, Swiss Chalet
09 Stuart House
10 Providence House.
11 Almshouses.
12 Weavers Tearooms.

Sibton.
13 Priory Remains.
14 Methodist church.
15 The White Horse Inn & Motel.

Heveningham.
16 Lodge Gates.

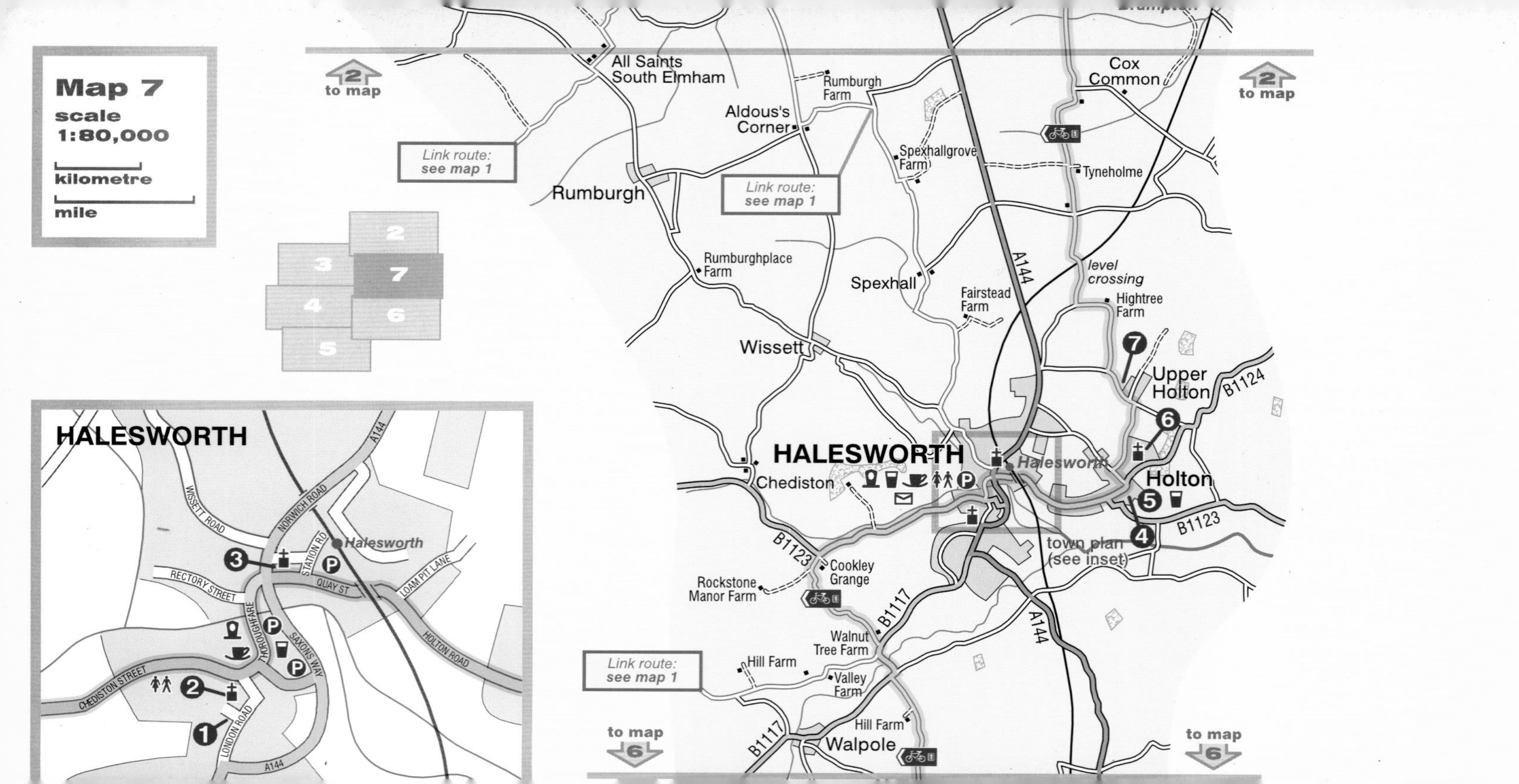
Map 7
scale
1:80,000
kilometre
mile
2
3
7
4
6
5
to map 2
to map 2
to map 6
to map 6
Link route:
see map 1
Link route:
see map 1
Link route:
see map 1
All Saints
South Elmham
Rumburgh
Farm
Cox
Common
Aldous's
Corner
Spexhallgrove
Farm
Tyneholme
Rumburgh
Rumburghplace
Farm
Spexhall
A144
level
crossing
Hightree
Farm
Fairstead
Farm
Wissett
Upper
Holton
B1124
HALESWORTH
Halesworth
Holton
Chediston
B1123
town plan
(see inset)
Rockstone
Manor Farm
Cookley
Grange
B1117
Walnut
Tree Farm
A144
Hill Farm
Valley
Farm
Hill Farm
Walpole
B1117
HALESWORTH
WISSETT ROAD
NORWICH ROAD
A144
Halesworth
STATION RD
RECTORY STREET
QUAY ST
LOAM PIT LANE
THOROUGHFARE
SAXONS WAY
HOLTON ROAD
CHEDISTON STREET
LONDON ROAD
A144

Halesworth

HALESWORTH

Halesworth is a small thriving market town on the main railway line between Ipswich and Lowestoft. It takes its name from the Saxon word 'halesworda', which literary means 'a corner of land enclosed by water on two or more sides'.

From the 13th Halesworth's prosperity grew and increased in 1761 when the Blyth Navigation was opened and allowed boats with keels to carry trade to the town. By the 19th century brewing and malting were the major commercial activities, and the town boasted 9 maltings.

Halesworth has been the birthplace to many famous and influential people, including Sir Benjamin D'Urban (1777), Governor of the Cape Colony who founded the city of Durban, South Africa. Sir Joseph Dalton Hooker (1817) the great botanist, author and traveller who like his Norfolk father became a Director of Kew Gardens. John Kirby (1690) and Henry Jermyn (1767), two famous topographers and George Lansbury (1859), the Labour Leader. Lansbury's father was working on the construction of the railway at the time, the family moved on when the railway was complete.

Holton Post Mill

The pedestrianised Thoroughfare has been pleasantly restored and is the town's main shopping street, lined with many interesting shops. Once a year along its length an antique market is held. Steeped in history the town has many fine houses of different styles and periods.

HOLTON

Close by its immediate neighbour Halesworth, Holton is built on high ground half a mile north of the river Blyth on the main Beccles road. Its principle historic features are a redundant post mill, a Norman round tower church and the remains of Holton Airfield. The ancient post mill was built by John Swann in 1749 and was working well into the twentieth century. Redundant, the machinery was removed and the mill buildings refurbished between 1966-8.

Like many ancient churches St.Peter's has been remodelled over the centuries but still retains the distinctive features beloved by its Norman builders. Its part Norman round tower stands 52 foot tall and its entrance is by a 15th century porch surmounting a Norman doorway. During the Second World War Holton Airfield was home to the 489th US Bomber Group, and was strategically important being only eight miles from the coast.

PLACES OF INTEREST

Halesworth .

01 Halesworth & District Museum.
02 St.Mary's Church.
03 United Reform Church.

Holton.

04 Windmill.
05 The Lord Nelson.
06 St.Peter's, church.
07 Airfield Memorial.

Heart of Suffolk Cycle Route

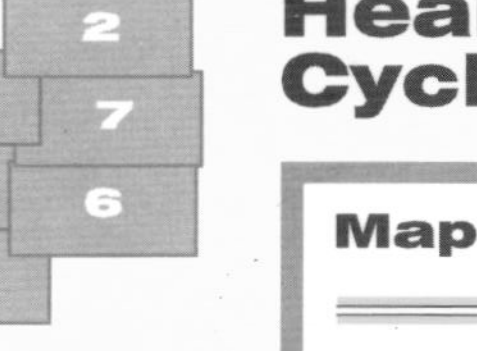

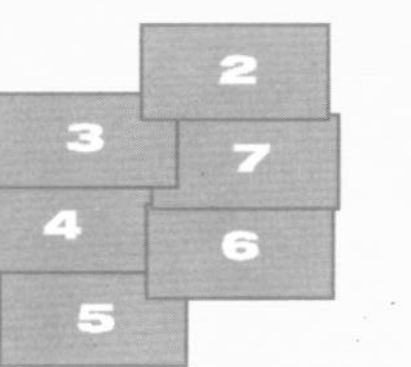

Map Legend

- Heart of Suffolk Cycle Route
- link route
- A road (A143)
- B road (B1062)
- unclassified road
- track
- railway
- rail station, station name (Brampton)
- built up area
- buildings
- woodland
- river, stream
- church, village sign
- shop, post office
- pub / hotel, café / tea room
- car park, public toilets
- point of interest on text pages
- point of interest on map only (St Mary's Church)

Route signs

- Heart of Suffolk Cycle Route
- National Cycle Network Route 1
- Suffolk Coastal Cycle Route

ISBN 0-86-055257-8

9 780860 552574